52 Smart Habits to Manage Your Money and Grow Wealth

Discover How To Improve Your Finances In 10 Minutes A Day

Joann Lindsey

Legal & Disclaimer

The information contained in this book and its contents is not designed to replace or take the place of any form of medical or professional advice; and is not meant to replace the need for independent medical, financial, legal or other professional advice or services, as may be required. The content and information in this book has been provided for educational and entertainment purposes only.

The content and information contained in this book has been compiled from sources deemed reliable, and it is accurate to the best of the Author's knowledge, information and belief. However, the Author cannot guarantee its accuracy and validity and cannot be held liable for any errors and/or omissions. Further, changes are periodically made to this book as and when needed. Where appropriate and/or necessary, you must consult a professional (including but not limited to your doctor, attorney, financial advisor or such other professional advisor) before using any of the suggested remedies, techniques, or information in this book.

Upon using the contents and information contained in this book, you agree to hold harmless the Author from and against any damages, costs, and expenses, including any legal fees potentially resulting from the application of any of the information provided by this book.

This disclaimer applies to any loss, damages or injury caused by the use and application, whether directly or indirectly, of any advice or information presented, whether for breach of contract, tort, negligence, personal injury, criminal intent, or under any other cause of action.

You agree to accept all risks of using the information presented inside this book.

You agree that by continuing to read this book, where appropriate and/or necessary, you shall consult a professional (including but not limited to your doctor, attorney, or financial advisor or such other advisor as needed) before using any of the suggested remedies, techniques, or information in this book.

Table of Contents

Introduction

This is the second book in the series, 'Smart 10-Minute Habits for a Better Life'.

The book aims to help you live a better life by achieving financial stability, happiness (by the fact that you will not have to worry about money), and harmony in life (by living life on your own terms).

The first book[1] discussed, in detail, the habit formation process, how your habits influence you, and how and why to form many small, 10-minute habits. The habits discussed in the first book aimed at helping you attain good health, wealth, happiness, and financial prosperity.

This book focuses entirely on helping you to use your money wisely, save more, invest, get out of debt, and achieve financial independence.

Renowned author Charles Duhigg once said,

"And once you understand that habits can change, you have the freedom and the responsibility to remake them."

---

[1] *Easy 10-Minute (or Less) Habits that Change Your Life:* https://www.amazon.com//dp/B08GZG4XB2

If you observe the pattern of your habits and the way they are formed, you will realize that you have complete freedom to make and break habits. The first book discussed this aspect in detail and taught you how to make and break different habits.

Now that you have that knowledge, you are all set to form all the habit patterns that can add value in your life, including financial independence. It is that one thing almost all of us seek in life.

It is imperative to achieve financial independence because it brings forth an enormous amount of freedom in your life. When you are not cash-strapped and stop living from one paycheck to another, you feel free to do anything you want. You know buying an extra bar of chocolate won't hurt your budget, and that you can now go on that vacation you always wanted.

Financial freedom feels great and relieves you of a great deal of pressure. That said, it is something you work towards slowly and gradually by building the right set of habits.

Just like you cannot lose 20 pounds in two days, you cannot become a millionaire, or whatever your financial goal is, in a few days. It would help if you nurtured this goal by giving it time and attention by building small habits that slowly yield compound results.

This is where the 10-minute habits come in handy.

In this book, you will learn helpful and easy-to-build 10-minute habits on how to:

- Manage your cash flow

- Increase your savings

- Reduce your spending

- Decrease your debt

- Improve your investment portfolio

- And grow your net worth!

As you progress with this book, you will also notice a remarkable progression in your money management and will experience notable growth in it, even if you've always thought inching closer to financial freedom is an impossible feat!

Without further ado, let us get started.

PS: Because we've already discussed in detail the basics of habit building in the first book in this 10-minute habits series, this book will not touch on the basics. Instead, it will focus primarily on 10-minute habits that will turn your financial fortunes around, for good!

The 10-minute habit approach is arguably the most effective approach to building lasting habits. The human mind works in mysterious ways. When you focus on any goal as a whole or see it spread over a long time, you become overwhelmed by it.

If you have to work out for an hour daily, and you have a sedentary lifestyle currently, you will naturally feel intimidated by even the thought of this idea.

However, if you only need to run or jog for only 5 minutes, that won't feel impossible. As you work on this habit for 5 minutes daily, you adjust to it and make it a part of your life with ease. Over the next few weeks, you start to engage in it regularly and slowly increase the duration.

Since it is difficult for most people to engage in activities that will enable them to manage their expenditure, save and invest, the 10-minute approach has been applied to this aspect as well.

Instead of trying to do everything, we focus on small habits that you can engage in daily, weekly, monthly, and even biannually to improve your financial stability and push you closer to financial freedom. With time, the little things you do add up and have a multiplying effect that you could not have achieved if you told yourself to do everything in one go.

Before you can build wealth, you MUST know where you are financially. This should be an ongoing activity if you want to stay on top of your finances.

That's why we will start by learning 10-minute habits that will help you to understand your financial situation all the time.

Chapter 1: 10-Minute Habits That Will Help You Stay On Top Of Your Financial Status

Irish philosopher and statesman Edmund Burke once said,

"If we command our wealth, we shall be rich and free. If our wealth commands us, we are poor indeed."

You can only direct that which you know inside out about. Similarly, you can only be wealthy and financially free if you have control over your money and spend it wisely.

To achieve wealth and abundance, you need to stay on the top of your finances and keep track of your financial status. This is necessary because it will help you understand how much money comes in and how much money goes out.

From then on, you can have a good understanding of your financial status and take appropriate action.

So which habits can actually help you stay on top of your financial situation? Let's discuss some of these habits.

#1: Create Your Personal Cash flow Statement

John E. Jones was right when he said, *"What gets measured gets done, what gets measured and fed back gets done well, what gets rewarded gets repeated."*

Similarly, it is only when you start measuring/tracking how your money flows/moves that you get to understand what will end up needing some adjustment and what sort of changes you need to make. You can then reward good progress and direct funds towards the positive things and 'punish' or redirect cash from things that you should not be spending money on.

Therefore, before you can even consider improving your financial situation, you MUST make it your priority to keep track of your finances to the very last cent. This should be an everyday thing – something you do every evening, morning, or something that becomes a continuous part of your everyday life.

There is no better way to achieve that than using a cash flow statement to keep track of your cash inflows and outflows, so you know where your money is coming from and where it is going. In so doing, you never have to wonder where the money went.

So what is a cash flow statement?

Well, a cash flow statement is a statement that shows how money moves in and out of your control.

By preparing your cash flow statement, you get better clarity about your income (cash inflows) and spending (cash outflows), and better understand whether you are handling your finances well. Ultimately, you get to know whether you have positive cash flow or negative cash flow. Cash inflows are basically all incomes – business profits, sale of assets, gifts, royalties, dividends, salaries, wages, commissions, etc. Outflows are all forms of payments or expenditures.

Plus, you figure out the areas of unnecessary spending, can eliminate them, and also reallocate your money, so you align your money with the meaningful goals in your life.

So how do you create a cash flow statement?

- First, measure how much money is coming in (your total income). Determine income coming from all your sources – business profits, salary, royalties, dividends, interest, side hustles, rental income, and other kinds of income. It does not matter whether the income is regular or irregular – note it down. Also, ensure you note down the specific dates when you are paid. Understanding where your money comes from, how much it is as well as when you receive the income is critical, as it can help you know how much money that you actually handle. If you have no idea about how much money comes in and when it comes in, it is very easy to make mistakes when budgeting.

- Measure how much money goes out, when the money needs to go out and where it goes to. Capture every expenditure, large or small, that you incur every single day – this includes both regular and irregular expenses. Your cash outflow comprises of the money you spend on yourself and your loved ones, money lent to people, investments you make etc., any activities you engage in, rent, utilities, and basic necessities of life. Ensure to write down the exact amount corresponding to every cash outflow.

You can use a journal (have a dedicated journal for your finances) where you have a long list of all your incomes from all sources (with short notes mentioning anything of importance) and another list showing all your expenses.

Spend 5-10 minutes every day or several times a day recording your cash inflows and cash outflows to ensure you don't have to wait for several days to recall what you spent your money on as this can easily make you not remember some 'small' or 'miscellaneous' expenses.

Every week, month or pay cycle, calculate the net cash flows by calculating the total for cash inflows and the totals for the cash outflows then deduct the total cash outflows from the total cash inflows.

Your cashflow statement can look like what's shown below:

Cash inflows		
Salaries	XXX	
Commisions	XXX	
Dividends	XXX	
Royalties	XXX	
Gifts from friends and family	XXX	
Rent income	XXX	
Side hustle income	XXX	
Total cash inflows		**XXX**
Cash outflows	XXX	
Rent/mortgage payment	XXX	
Telephone bills	XXX	
Electricity and water bills	XXX	

Transport expenses	XXX	
Car expenses	XXX	
Entertainment expenses	XXX	
Groceries	XXX	
Medical expenses	XXX	
Eating out	XXX	
Monthly shopping	XXX	
Other expenses	XXX	
Total cash outflows		**XXX**
Net cashflows (total cash inflows − total cash outflows)		**XX**

If the net cash flow is a big positive number, you are in a comfortable financial situation. This means that, with a little dedication, you can easily make changes that will set you on the path to financial freedom. However, if the positive is small, it means you are barely out of the woods and need to do much more to ensure you don't end up in trouble, financially, in case of an emergency.

If the net cashflow is negative, it means you are in financial trouble, as you are spending more than you earn – it means you need to put a lot more effort to get out of the 'red' and debt.

Make it your habit to fill up your cash flow statement with details showing where your money is coming from (every cent) and where it is going.

Tip 1: If you are using a journal, you can dedicate several pages to each item of the income statement to ensure you can capture every single item whenever it comes up (daily is best). You don't want to end up with a messy statement.

Tip 2: You can use a spreadsheet to make it easy for you to track your cash inflows and cash outflows (you can have one for your PC, Google Sheets, mobile device, etc.)

Tip: 3: You can use a specialized app or software to track your cash inflow and outflows. Some of the best cash tracking apps include Expensify, Concur, Wally, Quickbooks, FreshBooks, Clarity Money, Mint, Mvelopes, YNAB, etc.

When you keep track of your cash inflows and cash outflows, especially daily (this should really not take even 10 minutes to complete), it is easy to know how well you are doing.

#2: Prepare A Personal Statement Of Financial Position

A statement of financial position is simply a financial statement that outlines an individual's financial position at any specific time.

In addition to preparing your personal cash flow statement, as part of the process of knowing where you are, you need to prepare your personal statement of financial position i.e., a balance sheet. The balance sheet features a list of all personal assets and liabilities to give you a snapshot of how you are faring financially.

The balance sheet has a section for assets and another section for liabilities. If the assets are more than liabilities, you are considered to be fairing well financially. And if the assets are lower than liabilities, it means you are financing your lifestyle more using debt.

After preparing a balance sheet, you will have a good grasp of whether your assets are more than your liabilities or not and the extent to which you are in debt or financially afloat.

Moreover, from the balance sheet, you can tell whether you are financially healthy to the point of having assets that can pay any outstanding liabilities.

Also, from the figure you get from subtracting liabilities[2] from assets[3], you can tell whether you are living below your means, within your means, or beyond your means. You can then use this figure to decide where to direct your efforts.

So how do you prepare a personal statement of financial position?

Here is how:

- Create a list of all assets – note each one of them in one section

- Create a list of all liabilities – note them all in a separate section

- Total the assets and the liabilities

- Deduct the sum of liabilities from the sum of assets

---

[2] https://www.investopedia.com/terms/l/liability.asp

[3] https://www.investopedia.com/ask/answers/12/what-is-an-asset.asp

Your personal statement of financial position looks something like this:

Your Full Name			
Balance Sheet As At (Date You Are Preparing The Balance Sheet)			
Assets	**Amount**	**Liabilities**	**Amount**
Savings account balance	XX	Auto loan	XX
Checking account balance	XX	Mortgage	XX
Retirement account balance	XX	Credit card debt	XX
401K account balance	XX	Student loan debt	XX
Automobile	XX	Overdraft	XX
Home value	XX	Loan from	XX

		friend	
Investment Account balance	XXX	*Any other liability*	XX
Cash at hand	XX	*Any other liability*	XX
Investment in stocks	XX	*Any other liability*	XX
Any other asset that you own	XX	*Any other liability*	XX
Any other asset that you own	XX	*Any other liability*	XX
Any other asset that you own	XX	*Any other liability*	XX
Any other asset that you own	XX	*Any other liability*	XX

Total assets	XXX	Total Liabilities	XXX

PS: The value of the total assets and total liabilities MUST balance (or be equal).

#3: Set SMART Money Goals

You cannot expect to attain your financial goals without a plan on how you will go about it. While you may simply wish to be debt free and attain financial freedom, these are not enough to help you achieve whatever you want to achieve. You need to set SMART money goals consistently (whenever you are setting any money related goal) if you truly want to have an easy time.

By SMART, it means your money goal should be:

- Specific: Make it as specific as possible by clearly stating what you are trying to achieve. If you wish to have an emergency fund, state how much money you wish your emergency fund to have (how much worth of living expenses it will be) and how much money you will be contributing towards your emergency fund. The same applies to your retirement fund; how much money do you wish to have at retirement, and how much money will you need to contribute to get there.

- Measurable: Your goal must be measurable, as this is the only way you can tell whether you are making progress or not. If you wish to have $1 million at retirement, state it clearly and state how much money you will be contributing towards your retirement fund, e.g., $900 for 30 years.

- Attainable: It means that you should be able to achieve your target with the resources available to you. For example, all factors held constant, do you believe you can put aside $900 per month for 30 years? Does your income allow for that without straining you financially?

- Realistic and relevant: Your goal must be realistic and relevant to you. Don't copy-paste other people's goals into your life; make it personal depending on your specific life situation.

- Time-bound: Accompany your goal with a deadline, so you know its due date, and get started on it on time. In our example, 30 years may be the timeline for contributing to a retirement fund.

The SMART goal setting formula does not just apply to retirement – it should apply in every facet of your financial life, so be sure to use it whenever you are setting any money goals to set yourself up for success. It will really take a few minutes to set a SMART money goal, but the benefits will be tremendous!

#4:   Check/Review   Your   Financial Transactions Daily

Keeping track of your financial transactions every day helps you know where every penny goes, so you become aware of any unnecessary transaction and expense to mitigate it on time.

For instance, if at the end of the day, you realize you made an extra trip to the grocery store just because you forgot to buy a few essentials the first time, you understand the importance of making to-do lists to avoid unnecessary fuel and related travel costs.

This is just one aspect – keeping track of your financial transactions every single day will make it easy for you to spot when there is anything that needs your attention after noticing any undesirable trend.

It really should not take long to review your transactions – 10 minutes a day should be enough to review everything.

Whether you wish to keep track of your cash flows or balance sheet daily, weekly, or monthly, you shouldn't take a lot of time to prepare these (make sure to dedicate not more than 10 minutes to the activity per session).

After understanding your financial situation by looking into your cash flow statement and balance sheet, move to the next step to spot money leaks.

Chapter 2: 10-Minute Habits That Will Help You Spot And Seal Money Leaks

#5: Review Your Billing Statements to Stay Up-to-date With The Nature of Payments

Make sure your bank sends your billing and monthly bank statement to your email (if there is an online account, that's okay as well) so you can easily view it. Go through it in detail so you can identify any unnecessary or wrong transaction/ purchase that has been billed to your account.

Also, look for all the subscriptions to different activities, websites, and services that you have been using, such as Netflix, gym, etc. to make sure you are not charged for something extra.

Review all your active subscriptions to know which ones you are using. If there are any that you are not actively using yet you are being charged for, cancel the subscription. You can channel the money to something else.

#6: Review Your Credit Report

Another quick habit that gives you clarity on your finances is to review your credit report a few times a year to know your credit score. Your credit score is a figure calculated by assessing your credit history.

The higher your credit score, the more creditworthy you are, and the more affordable it is for you to access credit. Having a low credit score means that lenders view you as a high-risk borrower. While you may have something to do with your low credit rating, at times, the low rating may be contributed by errors within your credit report. As such, when you receive your credit report, you MUST make it your priority to check for the accuracy of every item in your credit report.

If you notice any errors, you should endeavor to have it corrected. You can search for books on how to repair your credit on Amazon to find books that will help you to improve your credit score.

One way to improve your credit score is to ensure you maintain your **credit utilization ratio below 30%.**[4] Credit utilization ratio refers to the amount of revolving

---

[4] https://www.experian.com/blogs/ask-experian/credit-education/score-basics/credit-utilization-rate/

credit that you are servicing currently divided by the total credit that you have access to.

#7: Pay off the Loans with a High-Interest Rate

When it comes to paying off your loans, try to get rid of those with a high interest rate first. Write down all your loans along with their interest rates on your financial journal, and arrange them in descending order starting from those with the highest interest rate moving to those with the lowest interest rate.

High-interest rates means that you are 'leaking' money unnecessarily. Seal those money leaks by paying off the loans that make you pay more in the form of interest and continue until you've paid them all, one by one.

Don't stop there; instead of paying your credit card payment in small installments, pay them off in a single go to avoid being charged for every installment you pay. Moreover, make a conscious effort to pay off your outstanding credit corresponding to your high-interest credit cards first to eliminate large sums of debt first.

The same applies to overdrafts – pay any outstanding overdrafts and commit to not use overdrafts, as they may not only affect your credit rating negatively but also make you 'bleed' money in the form of unnecessary interests and other charges. Every 2 to 3 days, go through your account details for a few minutes and review your daily spending. Assess whether you used an overdraft facility and commit to settling it as soon as possible.

It takes a few minutes to note down how much you are paying in the form of interest rates for different loans; make it a 10-minute habit that you do every week or month.

Tip: You could start a 'money-saving scheme' by adding $10, $20, $30 or whatever number you can afford comfortably in a jar every day. Slowly build on those funds to pay down the loans that make you lose the most money in the form of interest for every dollar borrowed.

Chapter 3: 10-Minute Habits That Will Help You Start Taking Better Charge Of Your Spending

#8: Have A Spending Mantra

A mantra is something you believe in and follow, just like a motto. It is important that you set rules and guidelines when it comes to spending your money. If earning a good salary and having a good job hasn't helped you save to date, probably, you need to work on your spending in order to save.

To save yourself from the problem, start having a spending mantra. This means you need to set certain rules when it comes to spending your money such as:

- Always save before you spend: Before making any purchase, and even paying for your rent, utility bills, and other things, save some amount of money.

- Question the importance of a purchase: Before making any purchase, analyze its significance and need for you, and only if you are sure it adds value to your life, opt for it.

- Set a certain spending limit for each day: Analyze your total expenditure and, based on it, set a certain spending limit for every day of the month. For instance, after doing your monthly groceries, paying your rent and bills, you should not spend more than $50 a day or even less. Keep track of your daily spending. If you observe a bigger amount flowing out of your pocket, figure out the unnecessary spending.

#9: - Budget Periodically (Every Income Cycle) And Track How Well You Stay On Your Budgets

Create a budget for a specific period (income cycle), and keep track of it by reviewing your daily expenses. For instance, you could create a budget for the week if your income comes weekly, monthly (if your income comes in every month), etc. You could also have a daily budget, which details how you will spend your money on a certain day.

The budget should detail everything you will spend the money on (you can have expenditure categories). Keep track of how well you are staying on the budget using the cash flow statement I talked about in habit #1.

There are different budgeting approaches, but one of my favorite approaches is using the envelope system of budgeting. With this system, you have an envelope for each category of expenditure, e.g., an envelope for transport, another for rent, another for groceries, etc. Whenever an expenditure item arises relating to a given category, you pick money from the envelope with the appropriate label, spend how much you need, then return any change in that envelope.

How to implement the envelope system:

1. **Decide the budget categories:** It is best to ensure all your money is budgeted for, so don't just have envelopes for a few categories of your monthly expenditures. You want to allocate all your money to something. So everything, including your mortgage payments, savings, investment contributions, transport, eating out, grocery shopping, gas, health insurance contributions, and more, should be included. Basically, if you spend money on something each month or at least regularly, make sure to budget for it during the specific expenditure period. Of course, bundle like items together to ensure you don't end up with too many envelopes that only prove confusing. Don't worry; even if you never get to hold the cash

(because payments go through the bank), just have an envelope for each expenditure item.

2. **Develop a budget for each expense item.** We've already talked about budgeting and using a journal to track your expenses so you know how much you need to allocate within a certain period. Use ideas from the 50/30/20 rule discussed below to ensure you stay within reasonable budgets for different expenditure categories. Of course, you want to make sure that you are on the same page with everyone in your household so be sure to involve them in creating the budget. All your net income should be allocated to something – savings and investments included.

3. **Have envelopes for each expenditure category** and write down the total monetary allocations within the period at the back of the envelopes. This will help you to know how much you've budgeted for each category by just glancing at the back of the envelopes.

4. **Withdraw cold hard cash for all the expenditure items** that can be paid in cash and keep the rest that needs to be paid through the bank in your account. Basically, you don't want to have any idle cash that you spend at your discretion. You shouldn't be going to the

bank to make any new withdrawals within an expenditure period (this will also help you cut on unnecessary transaction fees).

5. **Divide the money into the respective envelopes**.

    Note: Remember that you still have some envelopes with amounts written at the back, but you may not put money in them because the transactions go through the bank. Simply note down the transactions whenever they are effected.

6. **Whenever you need money for something,** pick the money from the respective expenditure envelope and spend it. If you have any change, return it to the envelope. You may also note down each act of picking money from the envelopes and returning change. Note at the back of the envelope or a document placed inside the envelope. It should take just a few moments but doing that will save you a lot of time and frustrations.

I like to combine this with the 50/30/20 budgeting rule. With this rule, you allocate:

- 50 percent of your take-home (after-tax) income to necessities/needs. In this case, needs are the things that are necessary for survival, i.e. rent/mortgage, groceries, utility bills, transport, healthcare, insurance, minimum debt payments, etc. If you are spending more than half of your income on needs, it means you need to do something to bring the figure down.

- 30 percent of your take-home (after-tax) income to wants: Wants are those things you spend money on that you may not necessarily need and can live without. Under this category, expenditure items include movie tickets, vacations, cable TV subscriptions, gym membership, the latest electronic gadgets, etc.

- 20 percent of your take-home (after-tax) income to savings: This category includes savings and investments.

As you would guess, the envelope system is very effective when you are shopping offline since you can easily carry the envelopes with you while going shopping. However, you will need to get a little creative to make it work for you when it comes to online purchases.

One way to do that is to note down the allocations per envelope within a given expenditure period. If you want to be more sophisticated, you can print a document showing dates and amounts, so you just fill the expenditures for specific dates - you will insert the document in the envelope – just fold it nicely.

Whenever you incur an expenditure related to a given envelope, just note it down on the respective envelope or the document inside the envelope. It may help to note down the running balance to ensure you know how much is remaining for each envelope.

Therefore, you will need to have a habit of noting down how much you spent with respect to different envelopes – it shouldn't take a lot of time (less than 10 minutes is enough).

Suppose you don't like the idea of carrying a lot of cash for whatever reason. In that case, you could make it work by having a blend between physical envelopes and cashless spending. All you will need to do is to note down in the respective envelopes whenever you incur expenditure (you can use apps like Goodbudget and EveryDollar to digitize everything[5]).

Tip: You can make this work very well if you have a dedicated household budget bank account. You fund the account at the beginning of every expenditure period.

#10: Plan Your Shopping Trips

Whether you are going for your weekly grocery shopping or going to shop for clothes, plan your trips. Avoid going on impromptu shopping trips because that often leads to overspending and messes up your budget.

Even if you make a sudden plan of shopping for something on that very day, give yourself a couple of hours before going out. Sit down peacefully for 10 minutes, and plan your trip to save your time, energy, and money.

- Think of what you want to buy, and why you need it. If you are going out for groceries, go through what you already have to analyze if you really need almost the same things again. If you have enough goods to last for a few more days, you may plan the trip for the coming week.

---

[5] https://www.penniestowealth.com/envelope-budget-system-apps/

- If you are going to shop for clothes, electronics, or a big purchase that would cost more than $200, assess its need and importance for you. If you are thinking of buying a laptop, go through your requirements, the options available, and the budget you want to dedicate to the purchase accordingly.

- Make a to-do list of all the things you wish to buy if you plan to buy more than one item during the shopping trip. This way, you try your best not to buy more than what you need and save money.

Once you plan your trip, go through your list a few more times to remember any important item or point. If you are going to shop with family or friends, involve them in the planning to make it exciting and fun for all of you. This way, you spend quality time with each other and create a good memory.

#11: Compare Prices For Big-Ticket Items And Shop At Different Stores For Your Monthly Shopping Until You Find The Cheapest Store

Before you can purchase any items that cost quite a bit, it is advisable to shop around and not just settle on the first store that you come across. You will be shocked by how much you can save.

Also, for your monthly shopping, try to shop at different retail outlets to get a feel of the different prices. Some outlets may have sales, discounts, and offers that can go a long way towards reducing your total monthly cost.

Therefore, rather than just being loyal to a particular brand, shop around until you find a store that is close enough and is relatively cheap.

#12: Assign an Activity to Every Dollar You Have

It takes a lot of hard work, sweat, and even blood (both figuratively and literally) at times to earn your income. Making money is never easy, but for some reason, most people spend it very easily, and that is exactly what strains their budget. The moment you get your salary or whatever income, assign an activity to every dollar you own. This way, you know the $100 you set aside is for your monthly grocery, $200 is dedicated to insurance, and so on.

There will literally be no money that is not assigned that you can spend in whichever way you want.

#13: Keep Money Meant For Spending Aside

Instead of keeping all your income in your bank account where you will simply be withdrawing or swiping your ATM whenever you need to incur expenditure, keep any money you've budgeted for spending aside. You can take it out and save it in an envelope, or put it in another account. This way, you don't touch your profit or extra savings and use money only from the budgeted amount. It takes less than 10 minutes to transfer the amount you have budgeted to spend in a certain period to another account or withdraw it from an ATM where you will put the money in envelopes.

Also, it is best to have two accounts, at least; one checking that you use for your budgeted expenses and a savings account where you keep your savings.

If possible, keep them separate in different banks that favor savings and checking accounts, respectively. The inconvenience that comes with using separate banks will be some sort of deterrence for impulse purchases.

Moreover, never mix your business and personal accounts; always have a separate account for your personal expenses and a separate one for all your business investments and savings. This distinction helps you keep the two aspects of your life separate to avoid any mix-up and confusion.

#14: Say No to Impulse Purchases

It is okay to buy a bar of chocolate, an ice cream, a can of soda, and anything else if you feel like it, but try to avoid impulse purchases that are too frequent. Buying something impulsively is alright if it is an occasional occurrence, but avoid making it a habit.

Suppose you had already decided to shop for some clothes for the fall season, but a pair of shorts captures your attention. In that case, you could think of how the summer season is ending, and you will not get a chance to wear it, even if it is 50% off. Reason with your temptations and present believable logic to distract yourself from meaningless purchases.

#15: Wait for 30 Days Before You Make a Purchase

Every time you have to make a purchase, especially for an item that is not really a need, pause yourself for a few days. It is best to wait for 15 to 30 days before going on with a purchase to figure out if you actually need that item or not.

Often, we buy things because they catch our fancy, and not because we truly need them. You may see an attractive pair of sunglasses, a lovely leather wallet, or a gorgeous dress in a store, and suddenly feel you need it; you start to think of all the situations and occasions that purchase will come in handy and feel a desperate need to purchase it. Before you realize it, you may fall for the temptation only to realize later that it was an unnecessary expense and a waste of money.

To stop having more regrets related to your buying behavior, wait for about 15 to 30 days or even more before going on with a purchase. If you think you need a new phone, wait for a month to be sure about it. You may likely forget about buying a new phone and start gravitating towards another purchase in that waiting period.

Similarly, if you feel you need to buy a new pair of shoes, give yourself a waiting period of 30 days and then go ahead with the purchase if you still feel strongly about the shoe after the waiting period. This applies mostly to 'wants', i.e., items you can really live without.

However, if you have only one pair of shoes and they are torn, it makes sense to buy a new pair of shoes immediately without waiting for 30 days.

#16: Be Proactive About Cutting Down Transaction Costs

In many cases, whenever you are making any financial transaction, you will pay some money to the card processor or your bank for enabling the transaction. This includes ATM withdrawals, payments, bank transfers and much more. If you have these transactions often, the amounts charged can actually add up to a significant amount over time.

You need to avoid that by withdrawing money in bulk and bundling transactions to ensure you don't lose money unnecessarily.

Check your bank or credit card statement to know just how much you are charged for different transactions. For transactions that you are charged, find creative ways to work around the transaction costs by, for example, bundling the transactions, so you are only charged once.

49

#17: Pay Bills On Time To Avoid Extra Charges And Penalties

If you are servicing any debt, credit cards, utilities, and automatic transfers, you should be careful to avoid being penalized for missed payments. If you don't pay on time, you are charged a penalty. What's more, these penalties and missed payments also affect your credit rating negatively, which means you end up losing more money in the form of higher interest rates.

You can avoid losing money unnecessarily to such penalties by paying on time and ensuring the originating account has money to fund any automatic payments/transfers. It takes a few minutes to check the due dates for different payments.

#18: Use Public Transport As Often As Possible

With Americans spending anywhere between $2,000 and $5,000 a year on transportation, it does not hurt to find ways to cut down on this cost. One way to do that is to use public transport.

While public transport can be a little inconvenient, especially when you have many errands to run, it can help you save some money, which can easily fast-track your journey to financial freedom by maybe paying down debt, contributing to your emergency fund, paying insurance premiums, etc.

Why do I say that, you may wonder? I have several reasons:

- For starters, gas costs money, and unless you are traveling with several people in your own car, you will end up spending more on gas compared to how much you spend when paying for public transport.

- Secondly, there is greater temptation to move around more when you are driving, something that ultimately increases your overall expenditure. For example, you will find it easier to travel to a new joint in town, out of town, or even out of state you've heard about when you are driving. While gas may not really cost a lot of money, the small 'extra' costs for gas will add up.

- You will also have to pay for parking charges in different parts, and probably have some tickets you have to pay and more.

- Having several cars, for instance, means you will have to be paying for insurance, maintenance, and other costs for the extra cars, something which definitely puts money out of your pocket. So unless you are already financially free, you really may not need the extra cars when you do an honest assessment of your financial situation.

All these seemingly small costs can add up over time and if you can save some, even if not all, you could easily get closer to the financial freedom you so much desire.

Therefore, analyze your transportation costs and find ways of cutting it as much as possible. It takes a few minutes to make the decision!

#19: Plan For Any Extra Or Luxurious Expenditures

Working on your expenditures, saving, and investing should not feel like you are depriving yourself. Therefore, it is okay for you to indulge in certain luxuries either weekly, monthly or how frequently you can afford. However, the key is ensuring that you plan for these expenditures and not engaging in impulse buying.

Therefore, each week or month, plan for those expenditures that are not necessarily things that appear every month in your budget. It could be that holiday you want to take later in the year, or that high-end restaurant you have been wanting to dine at or that toy that you want to buy for your child or that appliance that you want to purchase or that designer handbag. Whatever the expenditure is, ensure that you plan for it, and take some steps either weekly or monthly towards setting aside the money to cater for it to avoid having to purchase it using credit or using your savings.

#20: Shop Alone Whenever Possible

If you have kids, especially those below 15 years of age, it is best to shop alone. Kids are impulsive and are likely to have many demands during the trip, and sometimes you have no choice but to oblige to their demands that only harm your budget.

While it is fun to shop with family and friends, try not to do it too often as other people can easily influence your purchases and choices. You may want to buy a more economical shampoo brand, whereas your friend may suggest an expensive brand because they've heard it is a good one. That influence may cost you an extra $10, $20, or even more.

Making the decision to shop alone shouldn't really take even 10 minutes – make sure to make it a habit whenever you need to go shopping.

#21: Pay In Cash And Minimize Your Use Of Card

Whenever you shop, choose to pay in cash as this would save you the extra charge levied on your card if you swipe it. If there is a discount going on purchasing from your card, pay using your debit card.

If you need to use your ATM card to withdraw money, first look for an ATM machine of your own bank. Swiping your ATM card at another bank will incur you some additional fees that you really don't have to spend. Plan your ATM usage. If you cannot find an ATM of your bank near your house or workplace frequently, withdraw a big chunk of money once every week, two weeks, or a month to avoid unnecessary ATM transactions at other banks.

#22: Buy Things on Sale

End of season sales and sales on holidays such as Christmas, New Year's, and Easter are lifesavers. Even the biggest brands and companies put up their most expensive items at great discounts during sales.

That is the time when you should make most of your big purchases, so you get good discounted deals and save your hard-earned money as much as possible.

If you have to buy a new laptop, a washing machine, any electronic item, gadget, appliance, expensive dresses, make-up items, or anything else that would cost you less on a sale, and help you save anywhere from $50 to $100 or even more, wait for the right sale to arrive. Note down the price of that item without sale, and jot it down during the sale season to compare between the two prices, and analyze the amount of money you would save by buying it during the sale.

#23: Buy Quality Items

We feel very good when we buy something that we feel is cheap so we think we got a good deal. However, you need to ask yourself one question. Will that product serve my needs in the end, or will it end up being costly?"

Instead of just focusing on buying cheap items to save money, your focus should be on buying something affordable and good quality. Don't be tempted to purchase items just because they are cheap because sometimes, "cheap is expensive". Therefore, each time you buy something, evaluate the price against the quality to ensure that you get a quality item.

#24: Haggle Whenever Possible

Whenever you shop, try to haggle if possible. Negotiating an item's price and bargaining for a discount isn't being cheap. Instead, it is a wise move to save money so try to buy things from places where haggling is not frowned upon to bargain your heart out and save some bucks. Really, it takes just a few minutes to haggle. The difference between the discounted price and the sticker price may be quite significant.

Take this further by using coupons.

#25: Use Coupons When Possible

Most stores these days have discounts and coupons. Before placing an order for whatever item you are buying, ask whether they have any active coupons. If they do, the customer service representative will undoubtedly not fail to disclose that material information.

We love getting free coupons, discount deals, and gift cards, but often, all these tickets and coupons only rot away in our wallet and bag. If you cannot redeem a coupon, there is no point in getting it.

However, if you do have one, utilize it as soon as possible. Go through all the coupons, discount cards, gift cards you have and write down their details such as expiry date, offer, etc. in your journal. Use the journal to track when the coupons will expire and try to use them beforehand.

By using the coupons, you not only save money but also get whatever you wanted to get, which is a double win for you!

#26: Reduce Electricity Consumption

Electricity accounts for a good chunk of household expenditures for many people and even businesses. Luckily, you can take measures to lower your bill, even if you have appliances that use a lot of electricity like air conditioners, electrical heaters, washers, fans, driers, and ovens. You can adopt specific habits that help lower your electricity bill.

- Switch off the fans and lights in the rooms you aren't using.

- If you go to the bathroom for a shower, switch off the lights, appliances, and fan/air conditioning in your room.

- Do not keep phones and laptops on charging for a long time. Once they are fully charged, unplug them.

- Switch off your laptop/computer when you are not using it. The more it stays switched on, the more it drains the battery, making it necessary to charge it often.

- Switch on multiple lights in a room only when needed. If you aren't reading or working, keep only one light on.

Don't stop at electricity: use water, gas, and other utilities only when needed and as much as needed.

Tip: While you work on these guidelines, encourage your family members or people you share the space with to do the same.

#27: Engage in Cost-Effective Activities for Leisure and Entertainment

You really don't have to spend a lot of money to have fun and unwind! Just because you are having fun does not mean you should not bother with how much you are paying! Here are some ideas that will save you money when doing different entertaining activities:

- Instead of watching movies regularly in cinemas, watch those available on Netflix, or get a DVD and enjoy it with friends.

- While watching a movie, you and your friends can pool in and get takeout, or all of you can cook a meal each and have a potluck party.

- Instead of getting a sports club membership, you could have a picnic in the park, or on the beach, and play sports and games such as volleyball, tennis, rugby, etc.

- Go for a stroll, or cycling daily alone, or with friends to relax, unwind, have fun, and also stay fit at the same time.

- Get cost-effective arts and crafts supplies from One Dollar stores like the 'Dollar Tree,' and engage in interesting crafts alone, with friends or family members at home. You can have an Art Attack day wherein all of you create attractive and fun art with the supplies. You could paint pebbles (use them for decorative purposes), do leaf printing by painting different leaves (create wall art using them), etc.

- If you wish to learn to strum a guitar or play any other musical instrument, don't enroll in a formal/traditional class, and buy a new guitar. Rather, you could borrow one from a friend and use online tutorials to learn the skill.

- Instead of having dinner dates with your partner in fancy restaurants, prepare a gourmet meal at home, and enjoy it over candlelight.

You need just 5-10 minutes to brainstorm the activities you can engage in that would not involve spending any money. Make this a regular habit whenever you wish to engage in a fun activity.

Once you start incorporating these ideas into your life, you will brainstorm more ways to enjoy and spend quality time with loved ones without spending too much money.

#28: Eat Home-Cooked Meals

It is fun to dine out, and getting takeouts is very convenient, but if you do that regularly, you likely end up spending a lot of money that you really don't have to spend.

Keep eat-outs and takeouts as an occasional occurrence and cook meals at home as much as possible.

Get food items in bulk for a week, or two, and prepare meals in batches. You can freeze them for a couple of weeks, and enjoy them all week. Do that for a few weeks while keeping a check on your cash outflow, and you will find yourself saving a good amount of money by cooking and eating at home.

While cooking large amounts of food that you can eat for several days takes time, you will only spend a few minutes to warm the food for the rest of the time.

#29: Learn To Skip Ads Or Use Ad Blockers

In this day and age, where it is easy to track your online activities, you will find yourself coming across ads that target exactly what you have been looking for. Thus, it is very easy to find yourself purchasing something that you had not completely made the decision to purchase but were just toying with the idea just because you saw an ad.

To ensure that you don't have to deal with such and that you stick to your planned expenditures, learn to skip ads, or install ad blockers. It takes a few clicks to do that, and your bank balance will thank you for that!

In addition to taking better care of your expenses, so you don't spend more than you have to, you also need to build habits that can help you save more.

Chapter 4: 10-Minute Habits That Will Help You Save More

Financial independence does not just come with daydreaming. You have to put in a great deal of effort to increase your savings and grow your investment portfolio. This does take conscious and consistent time and effort, but if you start developing the appropriate set of small, 10-minute habits, you can achieve this goal successfully soon enough.

Here are some of the most helpful, easy-to-nurture, 10-minute habits that can do wonders for your savings and investment portfolio.

#30: Always Pay Yourself First

When you hear the term 'pay yourself first', you are likely to misinterpret it to mean to spend on yourself first, but that's not what it means.

'Paying yourself first' means to put aside money for savings before you start incurring the expenditure. You put this money aside to take care of your long term financial commitments.

When money comes in, what many of us think of first is to pay all the pressing bills, i.e., to incur expenditure. Putting aside money for savings is the last thing on our minds – we save what is left if any. You have to change that if you wish to set yourself up for financial freedom. Put aside money that can ultimately grow and get you out of the endless cycle of living from paycheck to paycheck and even take care of your financial needs in retirement.

Many of us have the habit of splurging on ourselves and making unnecessary purchases the minute our salary reaches our bank account. While it is alright to sometimes splurge or treat yourself to something you have wanted for quite some time, it is unwise to turn this into a norm.

Every time you receive income, set aside a certain amount as your savings. Experts recommend aiming for at least 10-20% of your income to go to savings. Therefore, strive to increase your savings to at least 10-20% of your income if you are not yet there. And if you are already saving 10-20%, it does not hurt to increase your saving as is comfortable for you.

To make it even easier for you, and to ensure you remain committed, you can blend this habit with the next one.

#31: Automate Your Savings

Automating savings enables you to turn savings into a monthly/regular expense. By automating savings, you are not erratic in your savings – you don't save what is left after spending but spend what is left after saving.

That's not all; automating savings:

- Helps you to save time that you would otherwise waste trying to save manually

- Enables you to save more over time (because you are consistent)

- And makes it easy to get out of debt

Therefore, set up a plan (you can agree with your employer or bank) to automatically deposit money to your savings/retirement account. With this approach, you will not have to struggle with putting aside savings because you start budgeting and spending what remains after saving.

You only need a few minutes to decide how much you will need to be automatically deducted from your income and deposited to your retirement fund or savings account. From then on, all you need to do is to ensure that the account from where the money is deducted has enough funds to ensure every savings deduction is effected.

Tip: You can take this even further by using round-up apps[6], which offer creative ways to save money. Round-up apps automatically save any spare change by simply rounding up the amounts you spend in everyday purchases. So if you spend $8.25, for example, the app will automatically save 75 cents into your savings account.

Therefore, if you've always felt that you need a lot of money to save something substantial over a long time, you will be amazed by just how possible it is to accumulate a significant amount of savings by saving 'change'. Some apps like Digit[7] use artificial intelligence to analyze your spending patterns, from where they make decisions on how much to put aside as savings automatically.

#32: Save All Your Tax Refunds

If you often have tax refunds, don't just waste it on purchasing meaningless items. Put it aside in a savings

---

6   https://www.forbes.com/advisor/personal-finance/the-5-best-round-up-apps-for-saving-money/

7 https://digit.co/

account, emergency fund, investment account, or IRA (whichever you feel is most appropriate for you).

It takes just a few minutes to deposit your tax refund to the appropriate account – don't fail to dedicate those few minutes every year to set yourself up for financial success.

#33: Split Your Direct Deposits

If your employer pays through direct deposits, ask your boss or the HR department if they accept multiple deposit accounts. In case they do, deposit some amount in your savings account, and some of it in your checking account.

In case they do not, set up recurrent transfers to your savings account to ensure you stay consistent in your saving. Once you have money in your savings account, you experience a natural, internal resistance to spend it. This can work to your advantage as it makes it easy to grow these funds and multiply them.

#34: Direct Any Subscription Cancellations, 'Idle Money', Income Increments, And Windfall Income To Savings

This one is pretty straightforward. If you cancel a subscription, either because you are no longer using it or because after evaluating your financial situation, you feel it is an unnecessary expense, make sure to direct the saved amount to your savings account, retirement account, emergency fund, college fund, etc.

If you've paid off your debt, don't start spending the amount you were paying as loan installment. Instead, be sure to set up automatic savings to ensure the 'idle' money has something to do – growing your savings.

If you receive a pay rise or start making more income from your business or from whatever other sources, don't increase your spending with the amount of money added to your income. Instead, start by increasing how much you put aside as savings with the increment.

Suppose your previous level of income was barely covering for your living expenses. In that case, you could use a small amount of the increment to offset any deficit you had (assuming you are not exaggerating how much you were in a financial hole). Make the most use of automatic savings as early on as possible (before you start finding excuses for why you cannot save a significant chunk of the increment). If you were contributing to 401k, make the most use of the contribution rate escalation tool if yours offers that.

The same applies to windfall income like bonuses, inheritance, proceeds from the sale of a property, etc. Direct a major chunk of it to savings by living as if you never received any extra income. Going out for coffee, dinner, movie, or anything else you consider celebration may be enough to celebrate.

You can put the extra income in high yield savings accounts for example.

#35: Leverage Your Employment Benefits

Employment benefits, aka 'employee benefits' are the extra benefits offered to you in addition to your basic salary when you work in an organization. The commonly offered employee benefits include life insurance, disability insurance, medical insurance, retirement benefits, fringe benefits, and paid time off. All these have some monetary value to them.

As such, if you have access to these benefits, you should make it your priority to make the most use of them, as this will essentially save you money.

For instance, if your employer provides medical insurance, you save on medical bills and so you do not incur out of pocket expenses, unless necessary on medical bills. And when it comes to retirement benefits, if your employer matches your contributions to 401k, you are essentially getting free money. The same applies to disability insurance, paid time off, and fringe benefits.

Know what you qualify for based on your employment contract and ensure you make the most of each of these benefits as and when needed. It may not take a lot of time to go to HR to ask about what is included in the different employee benefits you get. And if you need any clarification, you can always go back to ask.

For example, be sure to understand what your medical cover really covers so you know the extent to which you can use it to your benefit or for the benefit of your dependents. Some covers may cover dental and optical, for example, while some may not cover that.

Ensure that even when changing jobs, you develop the habit of learning more about the benefits to consider before signing the contract. Also, always keep abreast of any changes the organization may make about employee benefits so that you can take advantage of them as soon as possible.

#36: Look Out For Government Benefits

Government benefits are the different kinds of helpful and supportive services that the government provides.

In the US, the government offers various benefits, such as:

- Affordable rental housing (that covers public housing or support in getting rental assistance)[8]

- Unemployment benefits (benefits you can enjoy, even in some cases where you are working – yes, you will be amazed at what's covered under benefits so don't just assume you don't qualify just because you make some money)

- Financial aid for students (support and grants that can help pay for school/ college fees)[9]

- Food assistance (food programs that provide you with meals, food coupons etc. so you can get free food)[10]

- Support with paying your utility and other bills[11]

---

[8]   https://www.investopedia.com/government-assistance-programs-4845368

[9] https://www.usa.gov/benefits-grants-loans

[10] https://www.usa.gov/benefits

- Military benefits (offered to military members, their families and veterans)

- Pension as well as retirement benefits[12]

Ensure that you are always on the lookout for any government benefits such as unemployment benefits, free education, healthcare facilities and the likes so that you can take advantage of these benefits and you do not spend money on activities related to these areas and you can instead save.

It takes just a few minutes (less than 10 minutes) to research about the different government benefits available - you could make it a weekly or monthly activity. Dedicate just 10 minutes a day or a week to just learning about all the benefits available, so you know which one you might qualify for.

#37: Save Money Whenever Possible

Every time you feel like engaging in an activity that costs a certain amount or you wish to buy an item, ask yourself if it is essential. If your honest answer is a 'no', ensure you put the money somewhere (maybe in a piggy bank).

---

[11]   https://www.healthsherpa.com/blog/top-10-government-programs-for-low-income-families/

[12]   https://gogovernment.org/federal-health-retirement-and-other-benefits/

The assumption is; if you were willing to part with the money, it means you wouldn't mind parting with it by putting it in your savings account, so you don't spend it on something else. You would have spent it anyway, so you have to assume the money does not exist anymore.

If you want to buy a pack of gummy bears that costs $5 but change your mind in the last minute, drop a $5 bill in your piggy bank. This way, you slowly start to save more money and keep a check on your regular expenses.

#38: Track Your Savings Progress Religiously

Assuming you already have a goal of accumulating a certain amount on your savings account, investment account, IRA, 401k, college fund, or emergency fund, don't just stop at having automatic deposits. Be sure to check how well you are progressing periodically. You can check your accounts every month, weekly or biweekly, depending on how frequently you are depositing (the more frequently you make your deposits, the more frequently you should check your progress.

You can use an spreadsheet to make the tracking clear and straightforward; all you need is a column that shows the date, the pending contributions, and another for savings.

Whenever you make a deposit (even if it is automatic), make sure to update the spreadsheet accordingly.

It can look like what's shown below:

Date		Savings
	Start of 2020	$2,500
	Pending contributions	$500
1/15/2020	$500	
2/15/2020	$500	
3/15/2020	$500	
4/15/2020	$500	
5/15/2020	$500	
6/15/2020	$500	

Don't stop at savings only; move a step further by investing the money to make sure it grows and multiplies. The next set of habits will focus primarily on investing.

Chapter 5: 10-Minute Habits That Will Help You Invest Your Savings and Grow Your Wealth

#39: Write Down Your IPS (Investment Policy Statement)

Your investment Policy Statement (IPS) should detail how and what you will invest in. It should comprise of the following:

- Your investment goals

- The financial products and assets you wish to invest in

- Asset allocation along with asset classes

- Your investment timeline

- When you wish to rebalance your investment portfolio

Rebalancing is simply the act of returning your investment portfolio to the diversification level you started from. If originally you planned to invest 40% of your funds in stocks, 40% in bonds, and 20% in mutual funds, you should rebalance when your stock allocation grows higher than 40%. Rebalancing allows you to keep your risk exposure to reasonable levels by diversifying your investments in different asset classes and maintaining that level of diversification.

When writing down your IPS, stick to clear and concise points. Clearly mention what you wish to invest in, and why and how long you wish to maintain that investment. Your IPS serves as a solidified, written guide to help you out when you start with investing your funds and helps you stay put when the markets turn volatile.

It can take a little longer than 10 minutes to prepare your IPS, so begin with going through the plan daily for 10 minutes, and jot down your pointers. After a week or two of analysis, you can review the pointers and compile them to create a comprehensive IPS that will serve as your compass during your investment journey and help you stay on track.

#40: Move Any Money You Don't Spend Within 1-3 Months To Interest-Earning Accounts

Saving money is good, but you won't get rich by just saving – you want to make sure that the money you put aside is also making money. This way, you don't lose money because of loss in purchasing power and inflation. Talk to your bank to know which accounts are interest-earning. It should not take a lot of time to talk to your bank about that – even a call, text, or message to your bank representative should be enough to give you the needed information to make wise decisions.

Typically, savings accounts generate more interest than checking accounts, so ensure you don't keep the money you are not really using (emergency funds, savings for a certain goal, etc.) in a checking account. However, banks have different banking products, so ensure you talk to your bank to know which product best suits your situation. By choosing the right account for your needs, you could easily earn a significant amount of money in the form of interest.

If the interest generated also generates its own interest, you take advantage of the power of compounding.

Albert Einstein referred to compound interest as the 8th wonder of the world in his famous quote:

"Compound interest is the eighth wonder of the world. He who understands it, earns it. He who doesn't, pays it."

Compound interest is the interest calculated on your initial principal amount as well as the accumulated interest you have earned. By virtue that you are reading this, it is clear that you want to earn the compound interest and make the most of it.

One of the critical determinants of growth in the compound interest equation is time. The more time you have on your hands to give the principal and accumulated interest time to grow, the more you stand to earn.

Let me give you an example:

If you invest just $420 per month for 40 years (from 20 years to 60 years) at a rate of 7% per annum, you will have $1,115,703.21! That's assuming you have an initial opening balance of $420.

Compound Interest Calculator (Daily To Yearly)

Beginning Account Balance:	420
Enter the Monthly ▾ addition ($):	420
Annual Interest Rate (%):	7
Choose Your Compounding Interval:	Monthly ▾
Number of Years ▾ To Grow:	40

Future Value:	1,115,703.21
Total Deposits:	202,020.00
Interest Earned:	913,683.21

And if you opt to start at 30 years, saving the same amount, you will have 518,785.68!

Beginning Account Balance:	420
Enter the Monthly ▾ addition ($):	420
Annual Interest Rate (%):	7
Choose Your Compounding Interval:	Monthly ▾
Number of Years ▾ To Grow:	30

Future Value:	518,785.68
Total Deposits:	151,620.00
Interest Earned:	367,165.68

Yes, the extra ten years will be enough to more than double your portfolio! You would need to save about $900 per month for 30 years to make up for the lost ten years!

This clearly shows how much more you can save when you starting saving at an early age.

Instead of saving more money at a later age, start saving a little amount regularly at an early age. I already explained how to automate your savings to ensure you stay consistent, so be sure to make the most of that.

It does not really take a lot of effort and time to take advantage of compound interest – all you need to do is to do some research on which compound interest-earning accounts you can have access to then start. Of course, don't let your judgment be clouded by higher interest rates, as that may also translate to higher risk, which may mean you could lose all or a part of your portfolio. It doesn't hurt to contribute to multiple investment accounts that earn compound interest. What matters is that you start early to make the most of time as a factor of compounding.

#41: Each Month - Have A Minimum Amount You Invest

In order to grow your wealth, you need to prioritize investing. It is advisable to invest a certain amount every month, however small that amount may be.

Rather than wait until you get some windfall or when your income increases, invest however much or little you have every month. Usually, it feels much easier to invest for example, $500 every month than accumulating $3000 in 6 months.

Furthermore, if you don't invest the money right away, then you will definitely find usage for that money. In addition, the more you invest, the faster you are likely to grow your wealth and achieve your financial goals.

#42: Increase Your Retirement Contribution Whenever You Get A Raise

I know it may be tempting to use the extra money to buy things that you wanted, and you believe that you can do that now because you have extra money. However, this is not the best decision, and you could do much more with the extra money.

Did you know that by simply increasing your retirement contributions by only 1%, this could have a huge impact on your financial stability?

Let us look at an example to help you understand this better.

For example, let us assume that Ava gets an increase of 3% on her $45,000 salary. She has two options at her disposal:

1. She can enjoy the extra $112 in her paycheck

2. She can decide to invest the money in her 401 (k). Since these contributions are usually pre-tax, Ava can actually enjoy more from her raise by investing that money towards her retirement. Let's assume she has 30 years to retirement, and she is starting from zero. Let's also assume 401k has an annual return of 8%, and the employer matches 100%. In 30 years, she will have an extra $150,901 at an out-of-pocket cost of just $42,818.

Decide how much of your raise you want to invest in your 401 (k) or IRA, then transfer that money. If your employer can match that amount, then take advantage of this and grow your investments even faster.

Make contributions to 401(k) and IRA a habit – it doesn't take long to inquire from your employer about the same (10 minutes is more than enough).

Chapter 6: 10-Minute Habits That Will Help You Increase Your Income To Move Closer To Financial Freedom

#43: Declutter Your House, and Sell Stuff that Can Be Sold

This is pretty self-explanatory. We all have stuff around our homes and offices that we don't really need and some that we don't even use. You could turn these to money by selling them and putting aside the proceeds from the sale of such items in a savings or retirement fund. And if you have any loan, you can use the proceeds from the sale of the items you don't need or use in your house or business to pay off part or all your loan.

This brings about 2 benefits:

- You get a decluttered home/office space

- You make money that you can channel towards paying off your debts, saving for a goal or increasing your retirement/investment contributions

You don't have to dedicate an entire day to decluttering your home or office. Every week or month, dedicate 10 minutes to go around your house or office space identifying anything you don't use or need and put it away. You can have categories for the items as follows:

- Useful items that I can sell

- Useless items that nobody will need i.e., junk

Dispose of all the junk immediately and commit to selling whatever is useful and can be sold off. You can have a garage sale, sell on eBay, Craigslist, and different other platforms.[13]

Tip: If you are not sure whether you will need something or not, simply place it somewhere you won't see it and keep it there for about a month. If you don't remember to want to use it within that period, it means you don't need the item and can sell it.

#44: Create Multiple Income Streams

Did you know that the average millionaire has about seven income streams?

What then does this mean for you?

---

[13]   https://www.thebalancesmb.com/best-online-places-to-sell-stuff-4140754

You need to stop relying on one source of income but create multiple sources of income.

Having several income sources is beneficial in several ways.

- For starters, it enables you to achieve your financial goals faster because you have more disposable income,

- Secondly, you are not too exposed in case one income source fails because you have several to rely on.

So, how can you create multiple income streams? You could start a side hustle that does not require too much time to start but can earn you some decent income. For example, you could tap into your talents and offer certain skills in a freelance capacity.

Usually, most people are afraid of starting a side hustle because they think it will take too much of their time. The thing about starting a side hustle is you set the terms; therefore, it does not need to take too much of your time from your main source of income.

You could also think of setting up passive income streams like starting a blog, affiliate marketing, selling a course, dropshipping, self-publishing through KDP, among other things. Most of these activities just need a few minutes every day, and you can earn a decent amount of money each month.

Your goal should be each day to spend about 10 minutes looking for alternative sources of income that you can create because there is always something new coming up.

#45: Work On Your Time Management Skills

You can only declutter and sell the extra stuff and create multiple income streams when you have the time to do so. Therefore, improving your time management skills will ensure that you get your main work done while still having enough time for your side hustles and other businesses.

Each day, ensure that you have a to-do list that outlines the main activities you need to do concerning your main income source. Ensure you reduce your distractions by concentrating on work, taking short breaks to rejuvenate, and avoiding procrastinating.

Just as you have a to-do list of important tasks that you need to do regarding your main source of income, you need to have a daily to-do list that outlines what you will do that day to create an income stream – whether active or passive.

You can have a daily to-do list if you have time and if that is not possible, have a weekly to-do list where you assign the activity and the amount of time you need to dedicate to that activity to earn some extra money.

Chapter 7: Easy Habits To Protect Yourself From Financial Ruin

#46: Contribute To Your Emergency Fund

Having an emergency fund should be high on your priority list if you really wish to secure your financial position and possibly protect your investments and savings.

Think about it, when you have an emergency fund, you won't have to remove money from your savings account, investment fund, or even retirement account to solve the emergency. This is because the emergency fund provides what I call 'the first line of defense' during financial difficulties. It acts as some sort of shock absorber for any bumps you experience in life that may easily get you in debt or make you lose your retirement benefits.

You may lose your job, require a major car/home repair, get sick, and all manner of other unexpected occurrences that demand money. At such times, having an emergency fund can prove extremely helpful in providing the much needed financial cushion to go through the financial crisis without getting into debt.

The rule of thumb is to have at least 3-6 months' worth of living expenses in your emergency fund. The more money you have on your emergency fund, the better (you can even have up to 1-2 years worth of living expenses in your emergency fund). The coronavirus pandemic has proven that anything is really possible, and having an emergency fund that can last you for as long as possible won't hurt.

So how do you build an emergency fund?

Well, you should start by calculating your total living expenses (how much you spend in your household per month). Your monthly budget should help you to determine this figure, so it should not take a lot of time to determine how much you spend within each pay period.

After that, determine how fast you want to build your emergency fund so you know how much you should contribute each week, each month, etc.

After that, all you need to do is to make your contributions. You can leverage the power of automatic deductions to ensure you stay committed to the goal. You could even contribute to your emergency fund from side hustle income, from the income you get by selling off items you don't need, etc.

And even as you contribute towards your retirement fund, make sure you track your contributions and any accumulated interest to know how well you are doing. Even after you've accumulated enough funds in your emergency fund, don't just forget about it – review it frequently to track how it is accumulating interest.

Note: Remember, you cannot tell when emergencies will strike. Therefore, put the money where access to the money is not too easy to deter you from withdrawing the funds and using the money even when you don't have emergencies. Obviously, you should not just put the money meant for emergencies in an account that does not earn any interest – since the use of funds may not be immediate, you may not need the money to be readily accessible. You can deposit the money set aside for emergencies in a high-yield savings account, money market account, etc.

#47: Contribute To Different Insurance Products

In addition to having an emergency fund, you should make it your priority to have insurance covers to protect you against the risk of financial loss relating to different aspects of your life. With insurance policies covering different aspects of your life, your savings, emergency fund and investments will be greatly protected from loss in case an insured risk strikes.

Think about it; if you have something like car insurance, you will not have to incur out of pocket expenses to take care of repair costs in case of an accident, for example. And if you have a health insurance cover, you may not have to incur out of pocket expenses whenever you seek treatment for various ailments covered by your health insurance policy.

If you have disability insurance, you will not have to struggle financially since you will use payments from the insurer for a specific duration, as set out in your disability insurance policy document.

And suppose you have renters or homeowners insurance. In that case, you will not have to incur out of pocket expenses in case the insured risk strikes, as you will get financial compensation from the insurer.

How to execute:

Dedicate 10 minutes a day to analyzing the different aspects of your life that would suffer financially in case of the occurrence of different risks and create a list of these aspects. From this list, find if there is any insurance product that can protect you against loss in case of the occurrence of the stated lists. Just dedicate 10 minutes a day researching until you find something.

After that, talk to several insurance companies to know what risks are covered, what is not covered, the policy amount, contribution/premiums, and other points of interest then choose an appropriate insurance product depending on your needs.

You can then automate your premium contributions to the insurance provider to ensure you are consistent. All you will need to ensure is that the originating account has money.

#48: Say "NO" To Co-signing Requests

It is very tempting to co-sign someone (a friend, relative, colleague, etc.) to a loan. After all, we all believe they will pay the loan they are requesting. But imagine a situation where you co-sign someone who fails to pay, for whatever reason (even death). You would be screwed since you will have to pay the money borrowed.

It takes less than 10 minutes to say no to any co-signing request and you may protect yourself from years of regret and financial trouble if the worst were to happen and you find yourself having to pay money you did not even use, just because you signed on some dotted line.

#49: Diversify Your Portfolio

Every investment has some level of risk of loss; some have high risk while some have a low level of risk. Imagine a situation where you have invested so much money in a single investment vehicle only for you to lose everything, probably because the company closes shop, files for bankruptcy, etc. All your efforts, even if good, would have gone down the drain.

You really don't want that to happen. As they say, don't put all your eggs in one basket – stuff happens and you find them all broken!

You can stop that from happening by having your investments spread across different sectors and asset classes. For instance, you can invest in bonds, stocks, mutual funds, high-yield savings accounts, real estate investment trusts, real estate, a startup, high growth companies, dividend-paying stocks (like dividend aristocrats), etc. The list of things you can invest in is practically endless; what's important is to ensure you diversify so you have your eggs spread across different investment classes.

Remember the point I mentioned earlier about rebalancing your portfolio – use that point and this one to ensure you minimize your exposure to risk as much as possible.

#50: Take Care Of Your Health

Your health is your wealth. I am sure you know that all too well. If you are healthy, you:

- Won't have to spend money on medical expenses, even to the point of exhausting your medical insurance cover

- Will be productive and hence able to generate more income

These two reasons are enough to make you prioritize your health. As such, ensure you adopt everyday habits that make you stay healthy in the long term. Stuff like eating healthy, exercising, taking care of your emotional well-being, keeping off stress and getting enough sleep (7-8 hours) should help you stay healthy in the long term.[14]

It takes a few minutes to list the activities you want to make habits of but the effects on your long term health will be immense.

---

[14] https://familydoctor.org/what-you-can-do-to-maintain-your-health/

Chapter 8: Other 10-Minute Habits That Will Help You Fast-track Your Journey To Financial Freedom

#51: Break Negative Money Thoughts

Your beliefs affect the habits you form, the decisions you make, and the overall quality of your life. In this case, your money beliefs refer to the beliefs and views you have related to wealth and abundance that influence your various money-making approaches and decisions. Understand that about 90% of your mental activities occur subconsciously, which means that your money-related beliefs affect 90% of your activities pertinent to money.

You may think that your money-related beliefs aren't negative, but if you haven't been able to save and grow your money, it proves otherwise. To become financially stable, you need to get rid of your unhealthy money-related beliefs. For instance, you may think that money is dirty, evil, is difficult to make and grow, is always in short supply, harder to hold on to, goes away faster, and that it is a sin to have more money. The more you dig into your money-related beliefs, the more you understand how they have influenced your financial decisions.

It is crucial to have healthy money-related beliefs because your beliefs directly affect your wealth and quality of life. Instead of viewing money as something negative, and thinking of having more money as being greedy, think of how you can attain financial freedom by being wealthy. Money is a reality of life, so treat it as one.

Every day, set aside 5 to 10 minutes to practice money-based positive affirmations. Affirmations are suggestions you say. When you affirm something to your subconscious mind, it accepts it and makes you work towards that goal. If you say, 'I am rich' with deep conviction, you actually believe that and start to look for ways to become rich. When you practice such affirmations, close your eyes and visualize yourself being wealthy and financially independent. Soon enough, you will start working smarter and harder to achieve great wealth and abundance.

Here are some great money-related affirmations you can practise daily to have a better relationship with money:

- I am a magnet for wealth and abundance.

- I easily draw money towards me.

- Money flows very easily towards me.

- I am financially strong and independent.

- I save and use money wisely and that helps my wealth grow.

- I am rich and happy.

- I save money easily.

- I spend my money wisely.

Every time you practice these affirmations, do so with deep conviction and put on a smile. This makes you believe what you say, drawing positive experiences towards you that help you actualize that goal.

#52: Have Accountability Partners

An accountability partner is someone who helps you keep track of your goals, cheers you on during difficult times, and pushes you to achieve your goals.

To better accomplish your money-related goals, look for someone trustworthy who can serve as your accountability partner. He/she will keep a check on your money-related activities, making sure you use your money wisely, spend only when needed, and invest in profitable opportunities.

Generally, having an accountability partner is keeping a two-way relationship, which means both, you and your partner, help each other save and grow your money. When both of you are accountable to one another, you slowly grow financially bigger together.

This relationship works well when you have a trustworthy accountability partner who is invested in this process and has the energy and time to devote to keep checking up on you to know how you are doing. He/she must be honest, should not be scared of giving you an unbiased input, and not be influenced by your decisions, so he/she gives you authentic advice and tells you where you are wrong.

Once you find an accountability partner with these traits, you need to set an agenda for your meetings and every accountability check-in. The two of you must also decide on how often you will communicate, the medium of communication such as phone calls, emails etc., whether you will show him/ her your bank statements, and communicate your financial goals in-depth with him/ her so he/ she can give you honest advice, and such

Once these aspects are settled on, the two of you need to start meeting regularly and work towards helping each other grow financially.

You can dedicate 10 minutes each week where you give each other status updates regarding your progress. This will definitely need to be supported by dedicating a few minutes to journaling everything you do regarding boosting your finances so that when it is time for the meeting, you have specific things to report about. You can even create a shared document (think of Google Docs or Google Sheets), where you will each dedicate a few minutes a day or every 2- 3 days updating what you've done to move closer to your goals.

Conclusion

I hope this book has been eye-opening on the habits you can adopt to fast-track your journey to financial freedom.

The process is really simple:

- Adopt habits that help you understand your financial situation and spending

- Adopt habits that help you cut your expenses

- Adopt habits that help you save more of what you are already earning and what you may earn elsewhere

- Adopt habits that help you to invest your savings and grow them

- Adopt habits that help you increase your income so you can get to the next level

- Adopt habits that protect everything

- And more!

When you know which habits you are adopting, as covered in the book, you will find it pretty easy to grow your finances and attain the financial freedom you so much desire!

If you found the book valuable, can you recommend it to others? One way to do that is to post a review on Amazon. Reviews help spread the word out about your experience with the book so that others can make informed decisions. They also help me grow as an author. Please leave a review for this book on Amazon by visiting the page below:

http://www.amazon.com/review/create-review?&asin=B08L5G9MGT

Thank you,

Joann Lindsey

Resources

https://www.investopedia.com/terms/l/liability.asp

https://www.investopedia.com/ask/answers/12/what-is-an-asset.asp

https://www.experian.com/blogs/ask-experian/credit-education/score-basics/credit-utilization-rate/

https://www.forbes.com/advisor/personal-finance/the-5-best-round-up-apps-for-saving-money/

https://digit.co/

https://www.investopedia.com/government-assistance-programs-4845368

https://www.usa.gov/benefits-grants-loans

https://www.usa.gov/benefits

https://www.healthsherpa.com/blog/top-10-government-programs-for-low-income-families/

https://gogovernment.org/federal-health-retirement-and-other-benefits/

https://www.thebalancesmb.com/best-online-places-to-sell-stuff-4140754

https://familydoctor.org/what-you-can-do-to-maintain-your-health/

https://www.penniestowealth.com/digital-envelope-system/

https://www.daveramsey.com/blog/envelope-system-explained

https://www.lifehack.org/articles/money/automate-your-savings-9-easy-ways.html

https://www.thebalance.com/co-signing-how-to-find-a-co-signer-315537#:~:text=A%20cosigner%20is%20someone%20who,and%20effectively%20guarantees%20the%20loan.

https://www.getchip.uk/the-sauce/get-out-of-your-overdraft

https://investmentmoats.com/budgeting/personal-cash-flow-statement-complete-guide/

https://www.experian.com/blogs/ask-experian/credit-education/score-basics/what-is-a-good-credit-score/#:~:text=Credit%20scores%20are%20decision%2Dmaking,repay%20the%20debt%20as%20agreed.

https://www.productiveandfree.com/blog/31-habit-quotes

https://www.success.com/17-motivational-quotes-to-inspire-successful-habits/

https://www.success.com/19-wise-money-quotes/

https://www.developgoodhabits.com/money-quotes/

https://www.forbes.com/sites/ryanguina/2019/08/30/simple-ways-to-increase-your-investment-returns/#77cbc14e27ca

https://www.doughroller.net/investing/7-ways-to-improve-your-investment-returns/

My Other Books in This Series – 'Smart 10-Minute Habits for a Better Life'

Easy 10-Minute (or Less) Habits that Change Your Life: Become Fitter, Happier, Wealthier, and More Successful! (Smart 10-Minute Habits for a Better Life Book 1)

Do you want to fight flab and get fit, increase your productivity, get a rein on your finances, find career satisfaction and even just be happier?

Yet, do you find that you're never going to get started on fixing these issues and finding a turnaround?

Perhaps, it's the lack of time in the mad rush of everyday life or it could be just that it's hard to muster the willpower to change things.

But do you know that you could finally get things under your control and achieve results by just adopting micro habits that take no more than 10 minutes of your time in a day?

These are small actions that require only minimal time to perform, so you're much more likely to get started and keep going on them to change your life for the better.

Easy 10-Minute (or Less) Habits that Change Your Life spells out the many micro habits you can introduce into your daily living to get a handle on your pressing concerns. It shows how you can start small at under 10 minutes and naturally increase the time spent on the mini action to transform it into a life-changing habit.

<u>Inside the book, you'll discover these micro habits that you can undertake to live life anew:</u>

- Habits to get yourself physically fit and even shed some weight

- *Micro habits to love yourself and grow better, including why you need to adopt these habits*

- Habits to boost your productivity

- *Habits to increase satisfaction with your career*

- How you can hone your potential with this ten-minute habit

- *How spending ten minutes of your time on these mini habits can help you secure your financial future*

- Habits you can include in your daily life to have quality time with your loved ones

- *And more!*

With this book, you can work towards not just your health and money goals, but also a slew of other important concerns as well, so as to achieve a well-balanced, happier life where your needs for personal growth, work and family life satisfaction and financial security are met.

Don't miss out on this opportunity to get around your problems and live a better life.

Visit: https://www.amazon.com//dp/B08GZG4XB2 to get your copy NOW!

Smart 10-Minute Productivity Habits: How to Boost Your Productivity and Achieve Your Goals (Smart 10-Minute Habits for a Better Life Book 3)

Unfinished projects and missed deadlines can get you down.

Discover A Slew Of Targeted Strategies You Can Incorporate As 10-Minute Daily Habits To Increase Your Productivity And Set You On The Path To Realizing Your Meaningful Life Goals.

Do you often marvel at how a day can slip by without your having accomplished anything worthwhile?

Do you fret at how you never seem to achieve the targets that you have set and wonder at how you can never get down to crossing off the items on your to-do lists?

After spending time in deep research, author and personal development aficionado Joann Lindsey came up with a habit-building system to attack the root causes of our productivity problems such as commitment issues, subpar time management skills and distractions.

In *Smart 10-Minute Productivity Habits*, Lindsey shares a collection of 48 actionable tips and strategies to transform your unproductive day into one where you successfully checked off items on your to-do lists to accomplish objectives that are meaningful to you.

This book builds on the first book in the series *Smart 10-Minute Habits for a Better Life - Easy 10-Minute (or Less) Habits that Change Your Life*, in which Lindsey expounds on how you can start micro habits and keep at them to become fitter, happier, wealthier, and more successful.

Each of the 48 habits delineated in *Smart 10-Minute Productivity Habits* takes about ten minutes in your day to accomplish and can be built on to become a lifelong habit.

Inside, you'll discover:

- How you can build unwavering commitment to the goals that matter to you and thereby stay productive

- Habits related to planning and goal setting to clarify what you want to achieve

- How to forge killer-focus on tasks that will help you achieve your goals

- Habits to enhance your time-management skills so you will get more done in a day

- Habits to take your productivity to the next level.

- And much more!

Smart 10-Minute Productivity Habits is your habits-packed practical guide to boosting your productivity and actualizing your goals. If you like doable habits, clear-cut exposition and systematic approaches, you will like Joann Lindsey's accessible resource.

Buy *Smart 10-Minute Productivity Habits* to skyrocket your daily productivity today!

Visit https://www.amazon.com/dp/B08P5JKHCQ to get your copy NOW!

Forming Good Habits Through Journal Writing: 52 Journal Writing Prompts to Kickstart Habit-Building and Start Achieving Your Goals (Smart 10-Minute Habits for a Better Life Book 4)

Do you invariably find yourself starting a new habit with enthusiasm only to see it fail miserably in the end? Discover how you can leverage the power of journal writing to build good habits and make them finally stick.

Every so often, you take up a new habit with well-meaning intentions, but then you do not follow through with it so that you eventually abandon it and return to your old unhealthy habits. Author and personal development enthusiast Joann Lindsey had been there herself, and in *Forming Good Habits Through Journal Writing*, she delves into the subject of how you can forge a connection to the habits you want to build through journal writing.

Instead of your putting down unorganized and random thoughts, she suggests a slew of journal writing prompts to provide for more structure and direction in your journal writing to help you work towards your specific goals.

This is the fourth book in the *Smart 10-Minute Habits for a Better Life* series. It builds on the series' Book 1, *Easy 10-Minute (or Less) Habits that Change Your Life*, where Lindsey discusses how starting 10-minute mini habits is the way to go if you want to build good habits for the long run.

As she outlines in the book, it is quite simply a matter of starting small on a new habit and ultimately building it up to transform it into a habit that will stick to the end.

In Forming Good Habits Through Journal Writing, you'll discover:

- 10 journal writing prompts to help you discover yourself so that you can find your true directions

- 10 journal writing prompts to build meaningful goals on which you can base your plan for action

- 10 journal writing prompts to unlock your inner motivation and spur you on to engage in your habits

- 10 journal writing prompts to take meaningful action towards achievement of your goals

- 12 journal writing prompts to help you stick to good habits and your goals

Forming Good Habits Through Journal Writing is a value-packed resource for journal writing that is brimming over with 52 journal writing prompts to get you into targeted, purposeful action towards habit-building. If you like systematic approaches, succinct exposition, and practical content, you will like Lindsey's accessible exploration of journal writing.

Buy *Forming Good Habits Through Journal Writing now* to craft good habits, achieve your goals and live life as you want it!

Visit https://www.amazon.com/dp/B08R8ZK7XR to get your copy NOW!

36 Quick and Simple Habits to Stress-Proof Your Life: Discover How to Deal with Stress in 10 Minutes a Day (Smart 10-Minute Habits for a Better Life Book 5)

Life takes its toll on us. Stressful life events overwhelm our existence so much so that we invariably become frustrated, angry, and extremely anxious. Now, discover how you can whittle away the stress of daily living by simply engaging in easy 10-minute (or less) habits that have you confront the stressors in your everyday living.

We all know it too well—a heavy workload or too much responsibility at work, that overbearing boss, even worse the loss of a job, an increase in our financial burden, an annoying relative, moving to a new home, the demands of being a caregiver, etc.

The stress weighs down on us and daily life becomes a strain. Like everyone else, author Joann Lindsey has had her fair share of exacting pressures in her daily life and after giving it thought and study, she developed an efficient, comprehensive approach to combating stress.

She recommends in *36 Quick and Simple Habits to Stress-Proof Your Life* a slew of 10-minute (or less) habits that you can incorporate in your daily routine to manage stressful events and other pressures. As she explains in the book, it becomes more workable to get around daily stressors by trying on simple micro habits than attempting to tackle it all with a huge, demanding effort.

This compilation of stress habits is the fifth book in the *Smart 10-Minute Habits for a Better Life* series. It builds on Book 1, *Easy 10-Minute (or Less) Habits that Change Your Life*, in which Lindsey spells out how starting simple, micro habits is the way to go if we want to transform our lives for the better with good habits.

By starting small, we can more efficiently sustain the habit to eventually build it up to become a lifelong habit that we will stick to.

In *36 Quick and Simple Habits to Stress-Proof Your Life*, you'll discover:

- 6 simple habits to calm down your sympathetic nervous system and bust stress

- 5 habits to help you dig out the underlying cause of stress and nurture a positive attitude towards it

- 8 easy habits to help you stay organized enough to beat stress

- 9 self-care, de-stressing habits to keep your sanity intact and your self-esteem healthy and growing

- 8 cathartic habits and activities to counteract stress

36 Quick and Simple Habits to Stress-Proof Your Life is your smart, go-to resource of doable habits that will effectively guide you in grappling with stressful situations and other pressures. If you like short, succinct reads, practical solutions, and bite-sized action tips, you will like Lindsey's accessible and workable prescription for stress.

Buy the book now to get started on reining in debilitating stress and living life in peace, calm and happiness!

Buy 36 Quick and Simple Habits to Stress-Proof Your Life now!

Visit https://www.amazon.com/dp/B08V5RRN5H to get your copy NOW!

www.ingramcontent.com/pod-product-compliance
Lightning Source LLC
Chambersburg PA
CBHW070355220526
45467CB00001B/387